SOWER OF THE SEED

by Juli Camarin

ISBN-13: 978-0615841540
ISBN-10: 0615841546
ASIN: B00DLLD2GY

Project Editors: Dave Seawel, Sue Bussey

Cover Art by Juli Camarin.

A special thank you to Andrew Wommack and Andrew Wommack Ministries; awmi.net, whose great Bible teaching has influence me profoundly.

To my husband Hector,
Thank you for the freedom to study & write!

CONTENTS

SOWER OF THE SEED

MATTHEW 13:1-23; MARK 4:1-20; LUKE 8:4-15

As Jesus was walking with His disciples He asked them a question, "Who do people say the Son of Man is?" (Matthew 16:13). They replied with what they had been hearing others say, "Some say John the Baptist; others say Elijah; and still others, Jeremiah or one of the prophets" (vs. 14). Then Jesus stops and asks them a question that every one of us must face sooner or later...

"But what about you?" he asked. "Who do you say I am?" (vs. 15).

Jesus' first concern was that of the heart. He wanted the disciples to know and recognize Him for who He was. Peter, stepped up to confess that Jesus was the Christ, the Son of the living God, the Holy One of Israel and the One the world was waiting for and in need of (vs. 16). And Jesus called him blessed for it!

"Blessed are you, Simon son of Jonah, for this was not revealed to you by man, but by my Father in heaven. And I tell you that you are Peter, and on this rock I will build my church, and the gates of Hades will not overcome it. I will give you the keys of the kingdom of heaven; whatever you bind on earth will be bound in heaven, and whatever you loose on earth will be loosed in heaven" (Matthew 16:17-19).

As soon as Peter recognized and confessed that Jesus was the Christ, Jesus vowed to tell him plainly how the Kingdom of God works. The keys He gives are conventions; kingdom principles in which believers can and should operate. Jesus Himself confirmed this when He said, "whatever you bind on earth will be bound in heaven, and whatever you loose on earth will be loosed in heaven" (Matthew 16:19). The Amplified Bible gives clarity to this statement, "whatever you bind (declare to be improper and unlawful) on earth must be what is already bound in heaven; and whatever you loose (declare lawful) on earth must be what is already loosed in heaven" (vs. 19 AMP).

As believers we exist in the midst of two kingdoms, the earthly kingdom and God's kingdom. This is why Jesus prayed earlier in Matthew, "your kingdom come, your will be done on earth as it is in heaven" (Matthew 6:10). While we see and experience the physical world, we are not limited to it because we were translated to the kingdom of the Son the moment we believed (Colossians 1:13). As believers, we operate out of the heavenly kingdom which is why Jesus told the disciples that from then on, He would explain how the kingdom works. He promised to give them keys or principles so they could do greater works than He did (John 14:12). This applies to us as well.

As believers, we have the authority to bring into the physical realm the Kingdom of God. For example, if injustice is bound in heaven, then we can bind it on earth. If peace is loosed in heaven then we can experience it here in the physical. However, to experience and operate in these principles as they exist in heaven we must first know what they are and practice them. I believe Jesus spent a lot of time teaching on these and it is our job to know, recognize and work them.

Peter said, "His divine power has given us everything we need for life and godliness through our knowledge of him who called us by his own glory and goodness. Through these he has given us his very great and precious promises, so that through them you may participate in the divine nature and escape the corruption in the world caused by evil desires" (2 Peter 1:3-4). We have very great and precious promises that are unlocked by simply knowing and operating in them. This is a powerful and amazing truth, which is why Jesus first needed to know where the disciples stood concerning who He was. Once we come into that revelation, we are ushered into His kingdom, playing by His rules and given the keys to operate in it!

Throughout the gospels Jesus taught in parables. Fortunately for us, when He was alone with His disciples, He spent time explaining them. What He taught were Kingdom principles. By looking at these parables and their explanation we gain insight into the workings of the Kingdom.

Perhaps the most important parable to understand is the parable of the sower. Jesus confirmed this when the disciples asked its meaning, "Jesus said to them, "Don't you understand this parable? How then will you understand any parable?" (Mark 4:13). In other words, this parable is a key that unlocks the others.

THIS IS THE PARABLE FROM MARK'S ACCOUNT.

"Listen! A farmer went out to sow his seed. As he was scattering the seed, some fell along the path, and the birds came and ate it up. Some fell on rocky places, where it did not have much soil. It sprang up quickly, because the soil was shallow. But when the sun came up, the plants were scorched, and they withered because they had no root. Other seed fell among thorns, which grew up and choked the plants, so that they did not bear grain. Still other seed fell on good soil. It came up, grew and produced a crop, multiplying thirty, sixty, or even a hundred times." Then Jesus said, "He who has ears to hear, let him hear" (Mark 4:3-9).

The Amplified Bible puts it this way, "He who has ears to hear, let him be hearing [and let him consider, and comprehend]" (Mark 4:9 AMP). There is a truth so simple yet so profound in this parable that it is our job to hear, ponder, meditate and comprehend it.

SEEDS ARE KINGDOM PRINCIPLES

Before we dive into the explanation of this parable we must understand this amazing truth, seeds are Kingdom principles. Jesus uses the illustration of a farmer planting seeds because it is something we are familiar with and we can relate to. However, the seed itself is a profound truth.

In fact, the world's system operates on seeds. Without seeds everything would be barren and life would not exist. There would be no grass, no trees, no food and no people. God spoke the world into existence and with that, one of the first things He spoke into being was seeds. He produced seed-bearing vegetation, which has the ability to continually reproduce (Genesis 1:11-12). This is incredibly important, God created everything with the ability to procreate through the law of seeds. In fact, mankind was not put on the earth until this was done, otherwise they would have starved and life would have ended with Adam and Eve.

When Jesus revealed the Kingdom principle of the seed to His disciples it wasn't a new convention, this system was in place from the beginning. Jesus identified it and then explained to us how it worked so we can harness and use the principle of seeds in our own lives.

SEEDS HAVE GOD'S POWER IN THEM

Seeds can laid dormant for thousands of years and after mixing with soil and water will germinate and grow. This is because seeds are amazing! God ordained this law from the beginning and placed His power in them. It was so important that Jesus taught this to His disciples and commented that this principle was the secret to unlocking everything else (Mark 4:13).

We see this in operation in the natural all the time. Every year farmers plant crops expecting a harvest from the seeds they plant. In the same way, men and women procreate by seed. This principle works for believers and nonbelievers alike; because God set this in motion from the beginning. In the same way as in the natural, the Kingdom of God operates out of the principle of seeds. Which is why Jesus said, "He who has ears to hear, let him be hearing [and let him consider, and comprehend]" (Mark 4:9 AMP). There is power in understanding this truth.

KNOWLEDGE OF KINGDOM SECRETS

After Jesus finished teaching the parable of the sower to the multitudes and when He was alone with His disciples He took the time to explain it to them. However, before He revealed the meaning of this parable He started by telling them, "The knowledge of the secrets of the kingdom of God has been given to you, but to others I speak in parables, so that, "'though seeing, they may not see; though hearing, they may not understand'" (Luke 8:10). I love how the Amplified records this, "He said to them, To you it has been given to [come progressively to] know (to recognize and understand more strongly and clearly) the mysteries and secrets of the kingdom of God, but for others they are in parables, so that, [though] looking, they may not see; and hearing, they may not comprehend" (Luke 8:10 AMP).

People were coming from all around to listen to Jesus teach. However, because of the condition of their hearts they continually heard Him without listening, saw what He did without perceiving, nor were they willing to receive His message. He commented that a prophecy about them had been fulfilled, "In them is fulfilled the prophecy of Isaiah: 'You will be ever hearing but never understanding; you will be ever seeing but never perceiving. For this people's heart has become calloused; they hardly hear with their ears, and they have closed their eyes. Otherwise they might see with their eyes, hear with their ears, understand with their hearts and turn, and I would heal them'" (Matthew 13:14-15).

GOD'S KNOWLEDGE IS PROGRESSIVE

This is important, whoever has spiritual knowledge, they will be given more (Matthew 13:12). God's knowledge is progressive, which is why it is important for us to cultivate our hearts to see, hear, perceive and understand the Word. However, to those who refuse to listen and comprehend, even what they have will be taken away (Matthew 13:12). This is because these truths never have time to penetrate the heart, take root and grow. So in essence they'll never come into understanding or operation of this knowledge. And so it is lost, as a result, the life-changing, life-giving truths will never affect their lives. There is a great risk in not understanding God's Word.

Because what Jesus taught was the knowledge of kingdom secrets He spoke in parables to mask these truths to those whose heart was hard (Matthew 13:11; Mark 4:11; Luke 8:9). The King James Bible says the people's hearts were waxed gross (Matthew 13:15 KJV) Meaning they were extremely callous, insensitive and unreceptive. Jesus accused the multitudes in John, that they followed him, not because of the miracles that testifies to who He was, but because they ate the loaves and had been filled (John 6:26). Their hearts were continually hard and their motives were wrong. So Jesus spoke spiritual truths in parables so "though seeing, they may not see; though hearing, they may not understand" (Luke 8:10). He protected these truths from those who choose not to believe Him. These truths were the things that remained a mystery from the beginning of time but revealed when Christ came (1 Corinthians 2:6-8).

If the people would have desired to hear, understand and perceive what these things were, they would have turned to Jesus, and He would have responded to them with healing, forgiveness and insight.

BLESSED ARE THOSE WHO HEAR WITH THEIR UNDERSTANDING

Then Jesus turned to the disciples and said, "But blessed are your eyes because they see, and your ears because they hear. For I tell you the truth, many prophets and righteous men longed to see what you see but did not see it, and to hear what you hear but did not hear it" (Matthew 13:16-17).

For those who sought the Lord the outcome was completely different. He always took the time to explain what He taught. He gave them understanding and depth of insight. He told the disciples in the book of John, "The Spirit gives life; the flesh counts for nothing. The words I have spoken to you are spirit and they are life" (John 6:63).

This has application for us! Amazingly, we live in a time that many prophets and righteous men longed to see and never did. They only look forward in faith calling us blessed (Romans 4:6-8; Hebrews 11:39-40). Therefore, it is our job to take advantage of the time we live in, to listen, hear and comprehend the meaning of this parable; letting the truth soak in to change everything. Remember this parable is the key to unlocking everything Jesus taught, so it is crucial to understand and live.

THE WORD OF GOD IS A SEED

The primary explanation to this parable is the seed that the farmer sows is the Word of God (Mark 4:14; Luke 8:11). Since the Kingdom of God operates on the principle of seeds we must pay attention to the importance of Jesus' statement concerning the Word being the seed in this parable. This is the open door to understanding everything. The Kingdom functions like a seed; The Word of God is the seed that makes the kingdom work in our lives. As Kingdom people we must be Word minded, meditating on it to be continually planting seeds from scripture. It is a simple but profound truth.

GOD PLACES IMPORTANCE ON HIS WORD

The greatest gift God gave us outside of Jesus was the scriptures. He places incredible value on the Word that was written, preserved and passed down to us. It says in the Psalms, "You have exalted above all else Your name and Your word and You have magnified Your word above all Your name!" (Psalm 138:2b AMP). A statement like this makes me stop and ponder.

Paul told us in Philippians that Jesus was exalted to the place of honor and inherited a name above all else, at His name, everything bows and confesses His lordship (Philippians 2:9-11). Hebrews also starts out with this idea. Through His redemption victory, Jesus became far superior to the angels, just as the name He owns is far superior to theirs (Hebrews 1:4). Revelation tells us "On his robe and on his thigh he has this name written: King of Kings and Lord of Lords" (Revelation 19:16). In fact, when we are born again we make this confession of faith in His name and title as Lord (Romans 10:9-10). Finally Acts tells us "Salvation is found in no one else, for there is no other name under heaven given to men by which we must be saved" (Acts 4:12). Obviously God's name is extremely important, however, He magnifies His Word above His name, that's amazing!

JESUS PROVED THE IMPORTANCE GOD PLACES ON THE WORD

Everywhere Jesus went He used and operated in the Word. A great example of this is when John the Baptist was put in prison. Before this, John was convinced that Jesus was the Lamb of God. And freely gave up his own ministry and his own disciples saying he must become less so Christ could be more (John 3:27-30). Then, after being imprisoned by Herod and time had passed he sent his disciples to Jesus with a question. "Are you the one who was to come, or should we expect someone else?" (Luke 7:19). Discouragement and doubt crept in because of life's circumstances.

Look at what Jesus did in response to this question, "At that very time Jesus cured many who had diseases, sicknesses and evil spirits, and gave sight to many who were blind. So he replied to the messengers, "Go back and report to John what you have seen and heard: The blind receive sight, the lame walk, those who have leprosy are cured, the deaf hear, the dead are raised, and the good news is preached to the poor. Blessed is the man who does not fall away on account of me" (Luke 7:21-23).

Then after John's disciples left, Jesus turned to the crowd and gave a huge compliment about John, "I tell you the truth: Among those born of women there has not risen anyone greater than John the Baptist; yet he who is least in the kingdom of heaven is greater than he. From the days of John the Baptist until now, the kingdom of heaven has been forcefully advancing, and forceful men lay hold of it. For all the Prophets and the Law prophesied until John. And if you are willing to accept it, he is the Elijah who was to come. He who has ears, let him hear" (Matthew 11:11-15).

As John sat in prison, I'm sure discouragement crept in. It's interesting that this compliment by Jesus, about no prophet being greater than John, was given to the multitudes, not to John's disciples. Why? The answer lies in what Jesus did send back to tell John. As they waited for an answer, Jesus performed these miracles; He gave the blind their sight, He made the lame walk, He cured those who had leprosy and restored the ears of the deaf. Then He raised the dead and preached the good news to the poor. (Matthew 11:4-6; Luke 7:21-23). This is the message Jesus sent to encourage John while in prison in a dire situation.

At the beginning of John's ministry, the Pharisees came to him asking if he was the Christ. John replied in the words of Isaiah the prophet, "I am the voice of one calling in the desert, 'Make straight the way for the Lord'" (John 1:23). This is a direct quote from the prophet Isaiah. John found himself in the scriptures and knew this was about him, written five hundred years before he was born. John knew his mission was to prepare the way for the Messiah from this prophetic writing.

John was familiar with scripture and especially knew what Isaiah had written about the Christ. While John's disciples waited, Jesus performed everything that Isaiah said the Messiah would do in front of them and used this as proof to encourage John in prison. "Then will the eyes of the blind be opened and the ears of the deaf unstopped. Then will the lame leap like a deer, and the mute tongue shout for joy. Water will gush forth in the wilderness and streams in the desert" (Isaiah 35:5-6). He performed every one of these things in their presence and then raised the dead as the final proof, in case any doubt remained.

The takeaway point is this; Jesus did not stop at compliments to encourage John, it might have been said to the multitudes, however Jesus used the Word of God to encourage and confirm to John the answer to his question. He pulled out all the stops to make sure John had what he needed to survive in prison, locked up for Christ. Jesus wanted to reassure him that it wasn't in vain, He was the Messiah!

There is amazing application for us in this truth! If Jesus used the scriptures as the final and full authority on the matter, then planting God's Word in our heart is critical for success in life (Joshua 1:8). Everything we need for life is found in His Word (2 Peter 1:3-4). The trick is getting the seed inside where it can germinate and grow.

YOU NEED TO PLANT A SEED TO HAVE A HARVEST

The autumn following a move into the country brought with it a wonderful surprise; apples. As I walked my dogs around our property I noticed we had an apple tree and over the course of several months watched the process of this tree bear fruit. By harvest time, I had spent a lot of time thinking about its growth process; the result was a blog post from John 15 about remaining in the vine and producing fruit as a natural byproduct as part of that union. To sum up the feedback I received from my readers: It was a beautiful sentiment, without any concrete information on how to 'remain in the vine' and 'bear fruit'. (You can read the original post & comments here: jcblog.net/bearingfruit).

One comment in particular stood out because the reader wanted information on how to do this, however his caveat was that he did not wish for the answer of reading the Bible and praying. This is what he said, "You have given the classic answer of having relationship with God. Does this simply mean reading one's Bible and participating in what seems to be very one sided babble at an empty room. If that is all there is it seems a bit flat and one-sided and easily turns into works based "remaining in God".

As I prayed about this and how to respond, I asked the Lord for direction and insight on giving him something more than these things to help. His reply to me was direct, instant and something I already knew. The Lord said to me, "why would I give you another way, when I've already given you the best way!" God places such importance on His Word, that He would not substitute a relationship with Him in favor of some other less meaningful means of "remaining in him." Jesus said, "If you hold to my teaching, you are really my disciples. Then you will know the truth, and the truth will set you free" (John 8:31b-32).

As I thought about this, I became a little indignant that someone should ask me for practical steps on how to have a relationship with God and take away the power to respond by dismissing the validity of reading the Bible. The simple truth is that we need God's Word. Peter said, all things for life and godliness come through the knowledge of Him (2 Peter 1:3-4). Jesus said this was the key to bearing fruit in the very same passage about the vine, "If you remain in me and my words remain in you, ask whatever you wish, and it will be given you. This is to my Father's glory, that you bear much fruit, showing yourselves to be my disciples" (John 15:7-8).

YOU GET WHAT YOU PLANT

It's simple; you can't have a garden without planting a seed. In the natural realm we'd laugh at people expecting a crop without planting seed. The spiritual realm works the same way. We MUST plant a seed to have a harvest. Since the Kingdom operates out of the principle of seeds and the Word is the seed, we must be Word minded people, meditating and planting these seeds instead of the world's seeds.

The truth is that every word you hear is a seed; you are either planting life or death. Proverbs tells us, "The tongue has the power of life and death, and those who love it will eat its fruit" (Proverbs 18:21). Paying more attention to what the world says, what the media says, what the TV says will only give you death. If you continually plant those seeds, then of course you will live in fear and unrest. Paul said in Romans, "The mind of sinful man is death, but the mind controlled by the Spirit is life and peace" (Romans 8:6). In other words, to be carnally minded, controlled by the natural, will kill you. If you want peace you have to sow it. If you want intimacy with God, you have to sow it.

You get what you plant. Whatever you plant is what will be released and grow in your life. This is why we must be intentional about what we plant because the harvest comes from those seeds. By looking at what is being reaped in our lives, we know what was previously sown.

However, this truth has amazing applications for life. As an example, if you are sick, plant verses on healing and health. Meditate on God's promises surrounding it, give it time and this seed will release the physical substance for healing. Psalms tells us "He sent forth his word and healed them" (Psalm 107:20a). Proverbs says "for they [Words] are life to those who find them and health to a man's whole body" (Proverbs 4:22). In the same way, if you are struggling with guilt and condemnation, then plant the seeds of righteousness so you know how God sees you. Ephesians says, "and to put on the new self, created to be like God in true righteousness and holiness" (Ephesians 4:24). Paul said "There is now no condemnation for those who are in Christ Jesus" (Romans 8:1). There is a seed for everything you need.

Why does this work? Because "you have been born again, not of perishable seed, but of imperishable, through the living and enduring word of God" (1 Peter 1:23). The Word is incorruptible seed, it works each and every time, and every word contains life in itself! Everything you need is in God's word in seed form. If you plant it and mix it with faith, you will see results (Hebrews 4:2). The Word mixed with faith will produce a supernatural God kind of life, overtaking any situation you face. But to have a harvest you must plant a seed otherwise you will get weeds.

CHANGE YOUR THINKING, CHANGE YOUR LIFE

Proverbs 23:7 says as a man thinks in his heart, so is he. The core of what we believe will be evident in our lives. Changing our thinking, will change our lives. This is why we must renew our mind by the Word of God (Romans 12:2), so God's truth will be evident. This theme runs throughout the scripture.

Proverbs tells us, "My son, pay attention to what I say; listen closely to my words. Do not let them out of your sight, keep them within your heart; for they are life to those who find them and health to a man's whole body. Above all else, guard your heart, for it is the wellspring of life" (Proverbs 4:20-23).

Peter tells us, "His divine power has given us everything we need for life and godliness through our knowledge of him who called us by his own glory and goodness. Through these he has given us his very great and precious promises, so that through them you may participate in the divine nature and escape the corruption in the world caused by evil desires" (2 Peter 1:3-4).

Isaiah said, "You will keep in perfect peace him whose mind is steadfast, because he trusts in you" (Isaiah 26:3) or as the Amplified puts it, "You will guard him and keep him in perfect and constant peace whose mind [both its inclination and its character] is stayed on You, because he commits himself to You, leans on You, and hopes confidently in You" (Isaiah 26:3 AMP).

Meditating on the Word, planting seeds of life will give you peace. Sowing God's word and His thoughts about how to live and how to have a relationship with Him will naturally over take you and change your thoughts, your behavior and your life. Because this is a Kingdom principle, it is the same principle that grass, trees and people come from. You'll never get a crop unless you plant a seed. Believers can harness the principle of the seed as an agent of change.

The reply to my reader was exactly this, if you haven't been bearing fruit from your relationship with God, then start planting the seeds to do it. Intimacy comes through knowing who God is. And God has revealed Himself through Jesus and through the scriptures (Hebrews 1:1-4; II Peter 1:3-4). This is the way He has designed this relationship to function, you can't shortchange it in some other way.

A SEED WILL SPLIT A ROCK

We were discussing the Parable of the Sower of the Seed recently in the Bible study I attend. A friend observed when running through the trail system in our community, he's noticed seeds that have sprouted through the asphalt. He marveled at how this happens.

To the natural it seems backwards that a small seed can embed itself into a dry arid place such as concrete or a rock and start to grow. However the growth process is more dependent on the surrounding conditions than the seed itself. The seed will always work because of the power contained inside. Just as in the case of a seed growing out of a crack in the trail, when we plant the Word of God in our lives it has the power to split the hardest of hearts. It can grow and produce through the rubble and strongholds in our lives. A seed will split a rock!

THE WORD OF GOD IS ALIVE AND ACTIVE

"For the word of God is living and active. Sharper than any double-edged sword, it penetrates even to dividing soul and spirit, joints and marrow; it judges the thoughts and attitudes of the heart" (Hebrews 4:12).

The Word that God speaks is alive and full of power, which makes it effective. It can judge, expose and reveal the very thoughts and purposes of our hearts. And in the same way, it has the power to replace our worldviews with God's truth when we receive and let the seed take root.

This is because God watches to makes sure His Word produces. He told Isaiah, "As the rain and the snow come down from heaven, and do not return to it without watering the earth and making it bud and flourish, so that it yields seed for the sower and bread for the eater, so is my word that goes out from my mouth: It will not return to me empty, but will accomplish what I desire and achieve the purpose for which I sent it" (Isaiah 55:10-11). He told the prophet Jeremiah "I am watching to see that my word is fulfilled" (Jeremiah 1:12b). He told him that the Words He gave him to speak to the people would tear down, destroy, overthrow, build and plant and then placed the weight of fulfillment on His shoulders not Jeremiah's (Jeremiah 1:10).

There is a powerful truth in this idea. God's Word will work because He watches to make sure it is fulfilled. Planting His Word in our heart as an element of change is essential for the believer. Paul said that this has the power to pull down strongholds and make every thought captive that sets itself up against the knowledge of God (2 Corinthians 10:3-5). When applying this principle then, God's seed can split and crack the hardest places in our lives and change begins.

Everything you need is in God's Word in seed form. If you plant it and mix it with faith, you will see results (Hebrews 4:2). The Word mixed with faith will produce supernaturally because of this principle of the seed. The trick is planting the seed; Paul told us, "faith comes from hearing the message, and the message is heard through the word of Christ" (Romans 10:17).

The Word always works because the seed being planted is incorruptible. "For you have been born again, not of perishable seed, but of imperishable, through the living and enduring word of God. For, "All men are like grass, and all their glory is like the flowers of the field; the grass withers and the flowers fall, but the word of the Lord stands forever." And this is the word that was preached to you" (1 Peter 1:23-25).

Applying the principle of the seed guarantees success and progress in the kingdom of God, it guarantees result. In fact the Word is never the problem; it is how people react to it. It is always the condition of the soil that makes a difference in the harvest. However this truth remains; a seed has the power to penetrate the hard places in our lives, break them open, start to grow and change us as result.

THE SEED SOWN ALONG THE PATH

What makes the Parable of the Sower so powerful is the amazing truth about seeds. In fact, this is why Jesus explained this eternal truth in a parable and concealed its meaning from those who didn't believe. "Jesus spoke all these things to the crowd in parables; he did not say anything to them without using a parable. So was fulfilled what was spoken through the prophet: "I will open my mouth in parables, I will utter things hidden since the creation of the world" (Matthew 13:34-35). For those who trust in Him we are given in depth information on how the Kingdom of God operates so we too can work these principles in our own lives.

The Word is a seed; the seed will always work because of the power contained inside. However, the ground provides the seed with what it needs to grow and flourish after it is planted. In this parable Jesus describes four types of soil which translates to four different reactions to the seed. In this, we see that the condition of the ground matters in the harvest. The condition of the person hearing the Word determines the outcome, not the seed itself. The Word is never the problem; instead it is how we react to it.

THE SEED IS QUICKLY STOLEN

"A farmer went out to sow his seed. As he was scattering the seed, some fell along the path; it was trampled on, and the birds of the air ate it up" (Luke 8:5).

The first type of soil is the seed sown along the path. As the seeds are tossed on the ground, the dirt is so hard packed that the seeds are not able to penetrate the soil which means they lie on top and become bird food.

When Jesus explained this we learn an important truth, "Those along the path are the ones who hear, and then the devil comes and takes away the word from their hearts, so that they may not believe and be saved" (Luke 8:12). This is a scary situation; Satan has total access to steal the Word in this type of soil. Matthew's account adds clarity to this statement, "When anyone hears the message about the kingdom and does not understand it, the evil one comes and snatches away what was sown in his heart. This is the seed sown along the path" (Matthew 13:19).

There is great danger in not understanding. The evil one only has access to snatch away the seed if it is lying on the surface. In other words, the Word has to pass through our understanding. This is important. This is why we must present the gospel with simplicity and explain truths at a level where everyone can understand.

This is true when the gospel of the kingdom is presented as well as other truths from the Word. This does not only happen to non-believers when the gospel is presented. It can happen to us as well unless we keep our hearts sensitive to the Word of God. It is dangerous to become hard-hearted and not strive for understanding. We have many examples of this throughout the gospels where Jesus commented about hardness of heart. Most of the time it was about the Pharisees, or the people, however He said it to the disciples also.

A classic example is when Jesus walked on water, the disciples were terrified when they saw Him, and on entering the boat the winds died down and they marveled. However the scriptures record, "for they had not understood about the loaves; their hearts were hardened" (Mark 6:52). They had just witnessed Jesus feeding five thousand, but they didn't understand the miracle because of the hardness of their hearts. So when they saw Him walking on water they were afraid. The understanding of who Jesus was hadn't taken root in their lives at this point, the result was that this seed was stolen along with their peace in the situation.

UNDERSTANDING IS OUR FIRST DEFENSE

It is really important to understand the Word. This is our first defense; we must hear the Word with our understanding. So the seed can go down, be protected from plain view and have a chance to produce. The good news in all of this is that God has given us the Holy Spirit for this very reason.

Jesus spoke of this to His disciples, "When he, the Spirit of truth, comes, he will guide you into all truth. He will not speak on his own; he will speak only what he hears, and he will tell you what is yet to come. He will bring glory to me by taking from what is mine and making it known to you. All that belongs to the Father is mine. That is why I said the Spirit will take from what is mine and make it known to you" (John 16:13-15).

The apostle John took hold of this truth and wrote, "As for you, the anointing you received from him remains in you, and you do not need anyone to teach you. But as his anointing teaches you about all things and as that anointing is real, not counterfeit—just as it has taught you, remain in him" (1 John 2:27).

The Holy Spirit is a precious gift and one of His main functions is to teach and explain the truths of scripture to us as well as remind us of what Jesus said. There is also validity in having a Word mentor, someone to teach you from the Bible and train you in understanding it. And it is also why we have Pastors and teachers, to open up the Word of God to us. We have to condition our hearts to receive the seed with understanding. Otherwise you are leaving it out in plain view to be stolen.

In this parable the condition of the hard packed soil is the sole reason the seed is ineffective. It's never allowed to get beneath the surface where it can germinate and grow. The takeaway in all of this is that we must protect our hearts from hard-heartedness where the Word is concerned. We must keep it soft, pliable and teachable. We must plant these seeds giving them every chance to grow and produce. The harvest is dependent on the condition of the soil.

THE SEED SOWN ON ROCKY GROUND

I love tomatoes, so one spring I thought I would bypass buying plants in favor of starting my plants as seedlings. I bought the seeds and the supplies to do this. When I planted the seeds, I was amazed to see they sprouted within two days. However since I do not have a green thumb nor was I prepared for the life-cycle of seedlings, the plants died as fast as they sprouted because there was no room for growth... I didn't get them planted in the ground fast enough.

NO DEPTH OF SOIL; NO GROWTH

"Some fell on rocky places, where it did not have much soil. It sprang up quickly, because the soil was shallow. But when the sun came up, the plants were scorched, and they withered because they had no root" (Matthew 13:5-6).

The second type of soil is the seed that fell on rocky ground. Since the ground was shallow the seed started to grow quickly. However the soil could not sustain growth because there was no depth to it. So the seedling, when trying to weather the sun with no resource for moisture, withered quickly because it had no root system. Notice the end result is the same as the seed that fell along the path.

This is Jesus' explanation; "The one who received the seed that fell on rocky places is the man who hears the word and at once receives it with joy. But since he has no root, he lasts only a short time. When trouble or persecution comes because of the word, he quickly falls away" (Matthew 13:20-21).

In Jesus' interpretation we learn four things. First, unlike the seed sown along the path, this seed does penetrate the soil and grow. Secondly, the seed is received with joy. Next, it only lasts momentarily because of circumstances. Lastly, affliction causes them to fall away.

This is the person who receives the Word with gladness and gets excited but does not take the time to let roots develop. Just like the seedling, growth above the surface is quickly evident however; they will never produce because there is no depth of soil to sustain this growth. Because of this they are very vulnerable.

To make matters worse, during times of testing they quickly fall away (Luke 8:13). Jesus makes it very clear in this passage that persecution comes because of the Word (Matthew 13:21; Mark 4:17). Satan is the author of persecution and affliction in our lives. It comes for the Word's sake because he wants to steal it from your heart. If it's not laying on the surface to be stolen then he wants to tear it out before it gets rooted and established. It is much easier to root out a seedling than an established tree.

IT TAKES TIME TO DEVELOP ROOTS

To see the Word produce in your life, it takes time and you have to commit to it as a lifestyle. Effort needs to be put into getting rooted and grounded. Don't dwell on the visible results. Take the example of an oak tree, for every foot above the ground there is three to four feet of roots below the ground. By the time the seedling sprouts it is already well established. Then throughout its lifecycle, it withstands the storms because the strong roots make it stable. Put your effort into your root system. Get established in scripture and God will take care of the plume. Meditate, study, strive to understand and get some depth of soil. In the Christian life, visible results in life and ministry is a direct result of how deep your root system is.

The Word of God needs to get off the printed page and inside you to work. We need to get to a place where God's Word is more real to us than anything else. Paul understood this which is why he said, "Let God be true, and every man a liar" (Romans 3:4a). We must have this attitude concerning the scriptures. It has to be more important to us than our world views. It has to dictate our thoughts and actions. We have to decide that it is the absolute truth and authority in our lives. All of this takes time, which is a safeguard for us. However to have a harvest we must plant the seeds and give it time and room to produce.

SEEDTIME AND HARVEST

Here's the good news when planting seeds, they are working and growing even when we don't yet see results. Jesus explained this in the parable of the growing seed. "He also said, "This is what the kingdom of God is like. A man scatters seed on the ground. Night and day, whether he sleeps or gets up, the seed sprouts and grows, though he does not know how. All by itself the soil produces grain—first the stalk, then the head, then the full kernel in the head. As soon as the grain is ripe, he puts the sickle to it, because the harvest has come" (Mark 4:26-29).

There is a process to growth. First the seed is planted, then it sprouts, then a stalk appears, then the bud develops, then the fruit grows and is ready to be harvested. You can't cheat a seed, there is always a time element to it. However, we can have faith when planting that this process is working even when we don't see it or understand it because the principle of seeds is a kingdom principle. God designed it from the beginning to operate in this way (Genesis 1:11-13; Matthew 13:35). So we plant, we live our lives knowing that the seeds we've planted will grow and produce fruit if we give it the right conditions to do so.

THE SEED SOWN AMONG THORNS

Both my mother and grandmother are avid gardeners. They each have beautiful gardens that bloom all summer long. When I visit, we always spend time walking through the gardens to enjoy their beauty. However, those moments do not compare to the countless hours each of them spend working in them. To have a beautiful garden constant weeding is necessary otherwise the weeds will overtake the flowers.

THORNS CHOKED THE PLANTS

"Other seed fell among thorns, which grew up and choked the plants, so that they did not bear grain" (Mark 4:7).

The third type of soil is full of thorns. As the plants grow, the thorns also grow and choke the plants, robbing them of essential nutrients so they cannot produce. Notice no attention is given to weeding or removing the thorns, they are allowed to grow alongside the plant having access to the same nutrients and water supply. The weeds flourish, grow strong, overtake the plants and make them unfruitful.

Jesus gives insight in His explanation, "Still others, like seed sown among thorns, hear the word; but the worries of this life, the deceitfulness of wealth and the desires for other things come in and choke the word, making it unfruitful" (Mark 4:18-19).

This is how the Amplified Bible describes it, "And the ones sown among the thorns are others who hear the Word; Then the cares and anxieties of the world and distractions of the age, and the pleasure and delight and false glamour and deceitfulness of riches, and the craving and passionate desire for other things creep in and choke and suffocate the Word, and it becomes fruitless" (Mark 4:18-19 AMP).

This is the person who receives the Word; however the cares, worries, distractions and desires for other things are their main focus in life. Like a garden with both plants and weeds, there are only enough nutrients to sustain either the plants or the weeds, not both. In other words, where you place your focus is where growth will happen in your life.

A prime example of this parable in action is the rich young ruler. He came to Jesus asking what he must do to inherit eternal life. After a discussion, Jesus looked at him in love and said, "One thing you lack," he said. "Go, sell everything you have and give to the poor, and you will have treasure in heaven. Then come, follow me" (Mark 10:21). At this the man's face fell and he went away. He was very rich and the desire for wealth and worldly things trumped his desire to follow Jesus.

Having wealth and possessions is not wrong. And it appears that this man had a desire for God and sought out Jesus knowing life was in Him. His own words testified that He had made an effort to keep all of the commandments since he was young. Seeds had been planted; however, when it came down to it, the desire for wealth and the cares of this life, choked the seeds, making them unfruitful.

LIFE REFLECTS WHAT YOU'VE PLANTED

In the parable of the growing seed (Mark 4:26-29), we see that the soil activates the seeds (vs. 28). The soil will not only cause good seeds to germinate, it will cause bad seeds to germinate. Whatever you focus your attention on grows. Your heart brings forth fruit of itself (Proverbs 23:7 KJV). So careful attention must be given to the seeds you want growing in your life.

Modern day life is full of distractions. Busyness is a terrible enemy! We run from here to there filling up our lives with activities. Then when we are at home, it is easy to spend most of our time in front of a TV or a computer. By comparison, the time spent reading scripture or meditating on God's word is minimal.

By taking a look at society as a whole, we can see that we are reaping what has been planted. Everywhere you look you see violence, broken families and an entire culture that disregards authority. But look what is constantly on TV and it is no surprise these things have appeared in our society. The language and topics of today's shows would never have been acceptable to be on the air, even only ten years ago.

This same principle applies to our individual lives as well. Our lives reflect both what has been planted and what is given preference to grow. Weed seeds can be planted unintentionally by whatever we take in. Whether it is what we watch on television, the magazines we read or the gossip we listen to. A lot of seeds are tossed our way during the day. If we do not root them up right away then they are also allowed a share of soil in which to grow.

If the Word is going to make a difference in your life then you need to weed out other things. Jesus said, "The worries of this life, the deceitfulness of wealth and the desires for other things come in and choke the word, making it unfruitful" (Mark 4:19). To produce, the Word needs to dominate your thoughts, so for these seeds to grow we must get rid of the weeds.

HOW TO WEED YOUR GARDEN

Jesus started this parable by explaining that the Word of God is the seed. He went on to describe the different soils and different reactions to the seed. It is a progression. So here is an amazing application to this dynamic truth, if you let weeds grow wild they will sap vital nutrients from any scripture you plant. However, if you continually plant the Word, then it will choke out and overtake the weeds keeping them from producing.

This is done by being singular. In the third type of soil, they got too busy living and life choked the seed making it unfruitful. So we must stay focused. The Lord will cause you to prosper more than you can imagine if you stay focused on Him.

This is done by finding out what God's call and purpose for your life is and then giving your whole existence to that end. What is the one thing that God has called you to do? If you cannot answer that question then find out what that is and give yourself wholeheartedly to seeing that purpose come to pass. To be successful in that endeavor, continually plant God's Word in your heart and you will see it yield fruit year, after year, after year.

Paul said it is knowledge of God that demolishes strongholds and makes every thought captive and obedient to Christ (2 Corinthians 10:3-5). The Word of God is our offense to uproot and tear down anything that sets itself up against that knowledge. To weed, we must set aside the worries and desires of this world and give ourselves fully to the Lord. Giving more consideration to what He says, than any other source in our lives.

THE SEED SOWN ON GOOD SOIL

I grew up memorizing scripture from a very young age, our family and the church we attended placed a lot of importance on memory verses. This continued through my adolescence as well. While working at our church camp, the director encouraged all staff to memorize James 1. When that was committed to memory it was a natural progression to memorize other passages of scripture. By the time I was an adult, this type of learning had been a lifelong practice for me. Even now, it is not unusual to find me committing to memory the passages of scripture I am currently writing about.

The point is that these verses and passages have become a part of me. Learning them from an early age has helped me recall them quickly when I need them. The other advantage is the Lord reminds me of what they say when I am reading other passages, this brings fullness to my understanding. Best of all, since they are committed to memory I have the ability to think and meditate on scripture even when my Bible is not readily available. For me, memorization has played a key role in the harvest I am now reaping in life.

THE GOOD SOIL HAS LESS

"Still other seed fell on good soil. It came up, grew and produced a crop, multiplying thirty, sixty, or even a hundred times." Then Jesus said, "He who has ears to hear, let him hear" (Mark 4:8-9).

The fourth type of soil is the seed that is sown on good ground. When the seed is received it yields fruit multiplying thirty, sixty or even a hundredfold what was sown. Planting in good ground has an amazing return and is a surefire investment.

Notice that the seed is the same, however there is something special about the soil. This soil does not have more, it has less. Less rocks, less thorns, less hardness, less cares, less worries and less distractions so it has more room for the seed to work and produce.

When Jesus explained this parable He told us a few things about this type of soil, "But the one who received the seed that fell on good soil is the man who hears the word and understands it. He produces a crop, yielding a hundred, sixty or thirty times what was sown" (Matthew 13:23). So the elements to having good soil is hearing the Word and understanding it. Notice that this is the exact opposite of the first type of soil (the seed along the path), which are those who hear and do not understand, and the seed is quickly stolen (Matthew 13:19). Understanding is the key to producing in the kingdom.

In Luke's explanation Jesus gives another element to having good receptive soil, "But the seed on good soil stands for those with a noble and good heart, who hear the word, retain it, and by persevering produce a crop" (Luke 8:15). An essential truth to understand when planting is that the harvest does not happen right away, there is a time element to it.

Jesus explained this in the parable of the growing seed, "He also said, "This is what the kingdom of God is like. A man scatters seed on the ground. Night and day, whether he sleeps or gets up, the seed sprouts and grows, though he does not know how. All by itself the soil produces grain—first the stalk, then the head, then the full kernel in the head. As soon as the grain is ripe, he puts the sickle to it, because the harvest has come" (Mark 4:26-29).

The soil activates the seed and helps it to produce. Night and day, whether eating or sleeping the seed sprouts and grows. It takes time and we do not have to understand this process but rather, only know it is working when we do not yet see visible proof. Notice this process is the exact opposite of the second type of soil; in the soil with the rocky ground the seed grows quickly however since there is no root system to support the growth it, dies quickly (Matthew 13:6; Mark 4:6; Luke 8:6). So an important element to having a harvest is having patience and perseverance. There are stages of growth, it takes time to get this system working in your life, but in the long run it will pay off.

Jesus ends this explanation by declaring, "He who has ears, let him hear" (Matthew 13:9). Or as the Amplified Bible describes it, "He who has ears [to hear], let him be listening and let him consider and perceive and comprehend by hearing" (Matthew 13:9 AMP). Just as perseverance helps the harvest, listening, considering and continually understanding will also help the return. Notice this is the exact opposite of the third type of soil, which is the soil with the thorns. The thorns choked the seed making it unfruitful (Matthew 13:7; Mark 4:7; Luke 8:7). This is an illustration of life and letting the cares and concerns of the world occupy your thoughts and attention. These things will choke out the Word, preventing it from producing. However, Jesus said an element to having good producing soil is focusing, meditating and considering these truths continually. Listening so that you hear and understand, it is a continual process and it helps keep the weeds out.

PLANTING AND WATERING THE SEED

The Word of God is a seed and to be successful and prosperous in life we must plant into the womb of our heart and let it grow. How is this accomplished?

First, we must get the Word off the page and into our understanding. Paul tell us, "Faith comes from hearing the message, and the message is heard through the word of Christ" (Romans 10:17). So the first step in the process is hearing it. In other words, you must read it, read it out loud to yourself. Jot down questions you have about the text. Read it again. Talk about it with your friends. Think about it when you are driving. Ponder and consider what you've read. Pray and ask the Lord questions about it. Never stop reading it! Jesus said, "He who has ears to hear, let him hear" or another way to put it is let him hear, consider, ponder, meditate, mull it over, chew it up and perceive it. Spend some time in the Word and have both patience and perseverance with it. Perseverance, because it takes effort to settle and quiet yourself, entering into a place where you can listen and receive. And patience because it takes time to comprehend and understand. There is a process of coming into a revelation of scripture. Fortunately, from this parable we understand that the seeds are working even when we do not yet see visible proof.

Next, take encouragement knowing that the Holy Spirit is there to help you. In fact we have an unction from the Holy Spirit the moment we are born again. John tells us, "But you have an anointing from the Holy One, and all of you know the truth" (1John 2:20). His knowledge is deposited in our born again spirits, so we know the truth and it is the Holy Spirit's job to remind us of this, "But the Counselor, the Holy Spirit, whom the Father will send in my name, will teach you all things and will remind you of everything I have said to you" (John 14:26). This is one of His primary functions, "As for you, the anointing you received from him remains in you, and you do not need anyone to teach you. But as his anointing teaches you about all things and as that anointing is real, not counterfeit—just as it has taught you, remain in him" (1 John 2:27). So as you read take comfort knowing the Holy Spirit is there to remind and guide you into all truth.

Next, water the seed. It's amazing what a little water will do to help with the growth process. Did you know that the Word of God is both the seed and the water? "As the rain and the snow come down from heaven, and do not return to it without watering the earth and making it bud and flourish, so that it yields seed for the sower and bread for the eater, so is my word that goes out from my mouth: It will not return to me empty, but will accomplish what I desire and achieve the purpose for which I sent it" (Isaiah 55:10-11). God's Word is illustrated both by seed and water, so plant the Word and then water it by taking in more scripture and God is the one who will make it grow, "I planted the seed, Apollos watered it, but God made it grow. So neither he who plants nor he who waters is anything, but only God, who makes things grow" (1 Corinthians 3:6-7).

Finally, know that it is working because what is being planted is incorruptible seed, "For you have been born again, not of perishable seed, but of imperishable, through the living and enduring word of God" (1 Peter 1:23). The seed will always work; you can take comfort and encouragement in that!

THE RETURN; THIRTY, SIXTY, ONE HUNDRED TIMES WHAT WAS SOWN

One spring Sunday our Pastor was inviting people to participate in buying $20 worth of seed to be pooled together and given to a local farmer to plant. Then in the fall when the crop was harvested, it was to be sold and the proceeds used to buy food for those in need. The Pastor explained to the congregation what the average return was. As he described the amount of return this $20 worth of seed would bring in, my husband and I looked at each other because it was exactly the return that Jesus said it would be in the parable of the sower. That is the Word fulfilling itself. When you plant a crop on good soil it will yield a return of thirty, sixty, one hundred times what is sown, this is a kingdom truth.

RETURN ON INVESTMENT

"Others, like seed sown on good soil, hear the word, accept it, and produce a crop—thirty, sixty or even a hundred times what was sown" (Mark 4:20).

Jesus promises an amazing return on investment. If you take Him at His word and start planting the truth of the scripture in your life, He promises this seed will take root, grow and continually produce.

Throughout this parable we see a progression in the types of soil, which concludes with the soil that produces a return from the seed. It starts with hardness to the Word. The seed does not get planted, so it cannot produce. In the second stage, we might get excited about what we hear, but it's not really our revelation so the seed that has started growing, quickly dies. In the third type of soil, the weeds choke the seed making it unfruitful. This is an illustration of life's busyness, cares and worries, so again there is no return. However if the seed gets planted on good soil, then what is produced yields a return far greater than what was planted. That is the power of a seed.

In three out of four soils there is no return, the fail rate is great. However in the fourth type of soil, when there is a return, it is not merely a one to one ratio. In other words, you do not get one head of grain for one seed planted, you get multiple. This is an amazing truth; each seed that is planted and allowed to grow will yield in abundance. Plant a little seed, have a large harvest.

THE GREATER RETURN

As I was meditating on this I was curious about what makes the difference in the rate of the return. I thought about the difference between a tomato plant and an apple tree. A tomato plant is seasonal, you plant in late spring and it grows tomatoes all summer long. Put it in the sunshine being careful to water it and you will have an abundance of fruit.

An apple tree is also planted in the spring however you will not get any fruit from the tree that first year. In fact the tree will take two to five years before producing a single apple. During that time however the tree can grow between twenty and forty feet high. And when it starts to produce it produces year, after year, after year. According to a study done by the University of Illinois, during its lifetime, an apple tree will produce an average of 820 pounds of fruit. Another interesting fact about apple trees is that they do not self-pollinate, meaning to produce they need to be located by another apple tree.

When comparing the two I got a wonderful picture of the greater return. In both examples, the seeds produced, however the apple tree, took a long time to get established and needed a partner tree, but when ready, continually produced fruit every year. In application to life, this rings true. There are many wonderful truths that when understood and operated in they will continually produce in our lives. However the difference between the lower yield and the greater is patience and longevity. In other words, you must continually cultivate the Word that has been planted. Give it time to grow and surround yourself by other like-minded believers to encourage you in the process.

King David recognized this and recorded in the Psalm about the man who continually delights and meditates in the Word of God, "He is like a tree planted by streams of water, which yields its fruit in season and whose leaf does not wither. Whatever he does prospers" (Psalm 1:3).

Jesus said this is the key to a good return, "But as for that [seed] in the good soil, these are [the people] who, hearing the Word, hold it fast in a just (noble, virtuous) and worthy heart, and steadily bring forth fruit with patience" (Luke 8:15 AMP).

Thinking about this in my own life, I see the application of this truth. When I started writing through scripture, it was at a point in my life where I needed to draw healing from it. As I worked through the book of Romans, my heart responded to the grace expressed through Christ Jesus and everything changed. I didn't see myself as I was, I saw myself as who God says I am. Like the tomato plant, these truths started growing and producing quickly. They affected my worldview, my life, my family and how I interact with others. However, something unexpected happened as well, as I continued on this path of searching and studying the scriptures, taking the time to write and explain them so as to understand and know them, what I have written has blessed others. Years later, I continually get emails and comments of thanks about the truths I wrote so long ago. Like the example of an apple tree, these things continually produce year, after year, after year. Not only do they produce in my life, they have reproduced in others when they also understood the amazing truths from scripture.

This is an encouraging word, when planting God's Word and cultivating our heart soil, we know we will get a return. Through patience and longevity we can expect 100% return on the investment.

EVERYTHING CONCEALED WILL BE BROUGHT INTO THE OPEN

I had the privilege to co-teach an Ephesians Sunday School class recently. As I was teaching I asked the group a question to make them think deeply about the passage we were studying. I was interested in hearing their answers and the reasoning behind it. My intent was to challenge them, however in that moment of waiting while they processed, the Lord imparted to me a new understanding of the scripture concerning the question I asked. It was a deeper revelation than the understanding I had when I walked into the room. It was like a light bulb turned on in my head. I was so excited that I could barely wait to get home and search the scriptures to confirm what He spoke to me. I desired to study it out to prove and solidify this new understanding of the passage. I spent the next couple days looking into it. God's Word is progressive and He promises to bring us continually into a deeper understanding.

WHOEVER HAS WILL BE GIVEN MORE

"No one lights a lamp and hides it in a jar or puts it under a bed. Instead, he puts it on a stand, so that those who come in can see the light. For there is nothing hidden that will not be disclosed, and nothing concealed that will not be known or brought out into the open. Therefore consider carefully how you listen. Whoever has will be given more; whoever does not have, even what he thinks he has will be taken from him" (Luke 8:16-18).

Throughout the entire teaching of the parable of the sower of the seed, Jesus explains foundational truth about the Kingdom. It operates on the principle of seeds and there is an individual responsibility in the harvest. We must plant the Word and we must cultivate the soil to see a good return otherwise neglect will negate the seeds effectiveness. That is the principle, this is the point, "For there is nothing hidden that will not be disclosed, and nothing concealed that will not be known or brought out into the open" (Luke 8:17). Jesus explained this truth so when applied He could reveal mysteries hidden since the beginning of time.

Jesus spoke of this when teaching this parable, "But blessed are your eyes because they see, and your ears because they hear. For I tell you the truth, many prophets and righteous men longed to see what you see but did not see it, and to hear what you hear but did not hear it" (Matthew 13:16-17). Paul also taught this, "We do, however, speak a message of wisdom among the mature, but not the wisdom of this age or of the rulers of this age, who are coming to nothing. No, we speak of God's secret wisdom, a wisdom that has been hidden and that God destined for our glory before time began" (1 Corinthians 2:6-7).

Everything is meant to be revealed to the believer through the Holy Spirit. In fact, this is one of His functions. It is His job to teach us and bring understanding of the things of God (John 14:26; 15:26; I Corinthians 2:12-13; I John 2:20, 27). Quoting from the Old Testament Paul said, "as it is written: "No eye has seen, no ear has heard, no mind has conceived what God has prepared for those who love him" (1 Corinthians 2:9). And most people stop there because in their thinking this is a beautiful sentiment. God has a lot planned for us but who can know or understand it? However, I believe the main point of referring to this Old Testament passage is the next statement, "but God has revealed it to us by his Spirit. The Spirit searches all things, even the deep things of God. For who among men knows the thoughts of a man except the man's spirit within him? In the same way no one knows the thoughts of God except the Spirit of God. We have not received the spirit of the world but the Spirit who is from God, that we may understand what God has freely given us" (1 Corinthians 2:10-12). God's desire is to reveal His entire character and truth to us however this knowledge is so great and so vast that He reveals it to us in stages. This is why we must train ourselves to be skilled in the Word of God, this is the primary way He imparts understanding of Himself to us. He confirmed this to the woman at the well, "God is spirit, and his worshipers must worship in spirit and in truth" (John 4:24). We can worship God in many ways but unless we know truth, we can get off into a ditch very easily.

This is an amazing incentive to studying the scriptures as God promises to continually reveal Himself and His will to us through them. This is a promise, Jesus said, "I no longer call you servants, because a servant does not know his master's business. Instead, I have called you friends, for everything that I learned from my Father I have made known to you" (John 15:15). Paul said, "Do not conform any longer to the pattern of this world, but be transformed by the renewing of your mind. Then you will be able to test and approve what God's will is—his good, pleasing and perfect will" (Romans 12:2).

CONSIDER CAREFULLY HOW YOU LISTEN

"And He said to them, 'Be careful what you are hearing. The measure [of thought and study] you give [to the truth you hear] will be the measure [of virtue and knowledge] that comes back to you—and more [besides] will be given to you who hear. For to him who has will more be given; and from him who has nothing, even what he has will be taken away [by force]'" (Mark 4:24-25 AMP).

I am an early riser. I have found that if I get up very early when no one is awake I have the time and attention to focus on God's Word formulating my thoughts into written words. I have been doing it for years. However, some mornings are harder than others to get up. It's early and it's dark and sometimes I long to sleep in until it is time to get ready for work. On those days, it is not unusual for the Lord to place a verse or a worship song in head before my alarm clock bellows. As I struggle whether to get up or not, the desire to meditate on the verse or song overpowers my desire to sleep in and I get up. This is because I know from experience that God always meets me in those early mornings. It is a precious time where He teaches me and I enjoy the fellowship. In fact, I set a second alarm to notify me that I have to stop and get ready for work because in those moments it is easy to lose all track of time.

In this world, there are a lot of voices and we are inundated with many things. We have to know how to discern what is truth, even as we are flooded with the media, conversations and life in general. This is why Jesus said, "Consider carefully what you hear..." (Mark 4:24), and in another gospel it records, "consider carefully how you listen" (Luke 8:18), because the measure you use is the standard. With the measure you give, it will be given back. Give a lot of attention to what you hear and listen to from God's word and God will more than reward you for that. Give more attention to what you hear in the world, then the harder it will be to understand and receive the things of God.

The good news in all of this is that God honors and rewards those moments when we seek Him. His desire is to continually reveal spiritual truths to us. We have an amazing promise that can be applied to this principle as well as many other principles from God's word, "Give, and it will be given to you. A good measure, pressed down, shaken together and running over, will be poured into your lap. For with the measure you use, it will be measured to you" (Luke 6:38). God is a creative God and if you make the initial investment He will guarantee the return!

THE PARABLE OF THE MUSTARD SEED

"Again he said, "What shall we say the kingdom of God is like, or what parable shall we use to describe it? It is like a mustard seed, which is the smallest seed you plant in the ground. Yet when planted, it grows and becomes the largest of all garden plants, with such big branches that the birds of the air can perch in its shade" (Mark 4:30-32).

The parable of the mustard seed is well known. I remember many Sunday School classes where we were shown how small this seed is. Jesus points out that this seed when planted grows and becomes very large. The way it gets large is that it is planted, given time and the necessary nourishment and conditions while it grows. No one wakes up with a surprise mustard tree in the yard. If you plant it you'll watch it grow over time.

This is an illustration of how the Kingdom works. The Kingdom of Heaven is like a seed (Matthew 13:31; Mark 4:30-31). We receive this seed (or Kingdom) when we are born again. Paul said, "For he has rescued us from the dominion of darkness and brought us into the kingdom of the Son he loves" (Colossians 1:13). The King James Bible says that we were translated into the Kingdom. We once belonged to the kingdom of the world and now we belong in the Kingdom of God, where His rule and reign is manifested.

The Kingdom is so huge, so vast and so powerful that nothing can withstand it once planted and producing, however before this happens we must receive it in seed form. Peter said, "For you have been born again, not of perishable seed, but of imperishable, through the living and enduring word of God" (1 Peter 1:23). We might live our lives unaware of this Kingdom until we come face to face with the gospel of Jesus Christ, we receive this Word and this translation happens. The gospel is the seed that we need to plant. It might start off small with no one else aware that its been planted, but when it takes root and starts to grow then nothing can withstand it, not even the gates of hell (Matthew 16:13-20).

THE BIRDS OF THE AIR COME AND PERCH IN ITS BRANCHES

"Though it is the smallest of all your seeds, yet when it grows, it is the largest of garden plants and becomes a tree, so that the birds of the air come and perch in its branches" (Matthew 13:32).

In our example of the mustard seed, we see that when full grown, the birds of the air can come and perch in the branches. This is a different end result than what happens to the seed in the first type of soil. In that instance the seed falls on the path and the birds of the air devour it making it unfruitful. However, once the seed is planted and becomes the largest garden plant, then the birds only find shade, they don't find lunch. The birds are symbolic of Satan, trials and hard times.

Jesus said, "I have told you these things, so that in me you may have peace. In this world you will have trouble. But take heart! I have overcome the world" (John 16:33). Trouble happens in this world. The good news is that Jesus overcame and gave us His kingdom so we too can overcome.

Take Paul as an example, Paul had such a revelation of Christ Jesus that he was buffeted by Satan and persecuted everywhere he went. Paul refers to this persecution as a thorn in his flesh because everywhere he went Satan stirred up opposition to the gospel message. "To keep me from becoming conceited because of these surpassingly great revelations, there was given me a thorn in my flesh, a messenger of Satan, to torment me. Three times I pleaded with the Lord to take it away from me. But he said to me, "My grace is sufficient for you, for my power is made perfect in weakness." Therefore I will boast all the more gladly about my weaknesses, so that Christ's power may rest on me. That is why, for Christ's sake, I delight in weaknesses, in insults, in hardshps, in persecutions, in difficulties. For when I am weak, then I am strong" (2 Corinthians 12:7-10).

Paul pleaded with the Lord to do something about it; however God's response was "My grace is sufficient for you" (vs. 9a). It took Paul three times of asking for help before he listened. God's grace is enough to deal with Satan and his kingdom. Understanding God's grace gives you the power to overcome certain things. James said, "Submit yourselves, then, to God. Resist the devil, and he will flee from you" (James 4:7). Why will he flee from you? Because he is a defeated foe and cannot tell the difference between the believer and Jesus (Colossians 2:15). Isaiah prophesied what the Messiah would look like when He came to redeem mankind, "He put on righteousness as his breastplate, and the helmet of salvation on his head" (Isaiah 59:17). This is pretty much the description that Paul gives of the believer in Ephesians 6, "Stand firm then, with the belt of truth buckled around your waist, with the breastplate of righteousness in place, and with your feet fitted with the readiness that comes from the gospel of peace. In addition to all this, take up the shield of faith, with which you can extinguish all the flaming arrows of the evil one. Take the helmet of salvation and the sword of the Spirit, which is the word of God" (Ephesians 6:14-17). When Paul finally understood what God was saying, he took care of the situation himself as demonstrated in the very last words in the book of Acts, "For two whole years Paul stayed there in his own rented house and welcomed all who came to see him. Boldly and without hindrance he preached the kingdom of God and taught about the Lord Jesus Christ" (Acts 28:30-31).

Paul learned the secret, which is being strong in the Lord, using His grace, His power, operating out of His Kingdom and the authority given to the believer to withstand difficult times. This is the message he gives to the church, "Finally, be strong in the Lord and in his mighty power. Put on the full armor of God, so that you can take your stand against the devil's schemes" (Ephesians 6:10-11). He learned this by understanding the full extent of God's grace and how it works, "But He said to me, My grace (My favor and loving-kindness and mercy) is enough for you [sufficient against any danger and enables you to bear the trouble manfully]; for My strength and power are made perfect (fulfilled and completed) and show themselves most effective in [your] weakness. Therefore, I will all the more gladly glory in my weaknesses and infirmities, that the strength and power of Christ (the Messiah) may rest (yes, may pitch a tent over and dwell) upon me!" (2 Corinthians 12:9 AMP). Paul learned that He wasn't alone, God's power, God's kingdom and God's strength was available in these situations.

This is the power of the Kingdom. It is like a seed, you take it, you plant it, and it grows and flourishes. When the understanding of how it works comes, we learn that not even the gates of hell can withstand it. We can rest assured that difficult times will come, however what starts out small will become large and powerful so that these things will not shake us. These are the spiritual truths that Jesus teaches about the Kingdom of God. It is a seed, it is the Word of God and it has the ability to grow to such a degree that the birds of the air can perch and find shade, in other words they can do nothing against it once it is rooted in your life.

ABOUT JULI

Juli teaches the Word of God by combining humor, relatability, and depth in her messages. Her passion is for spreading the gospel of Jesus while helping His followers to understand who we all are in Christ.

Juli has been writing since a young age. The practice of journaling scriptural insights started during her sophomore year in high school as quiet time devotions. Since then, this habit of studying and writing on the scriptures has become a lifelong learning journey.

Juli is a active blogger and JCBlog.net is dedicated to explaining scripture through personal stories and anecdotes. She writes in a conversational way as she guides her readers verse by verse through the Bible. Her blog is widely read throughout the world.

Juli lives in Iowa with her husband. The couple has one daughter. In her free time, Juli is an avid reader, loves to run, enjoys cooking and spending time with her family. Read more about her at jcblog.net/juli-camarin.

This book, and others like it are available
online at jcblog.net/books.

www.ingramcontent.com/pod-product-compliance
Lightning Source LLC
Chambersburg PA
CBHW060610030426

42337CB00018B/3019